The Life of

a Boy with

Big Dreams

I have tried to recreate events, locales and conversations from my memories of them. In order to maintain their anonymity in some instances I have changed or omitted the names of individuals and places, I may have changed or omitted some identifying characteristics and details such as physical properties, occupations and places of residence.

Book layout by
Phyl Campbell, Creative Writing Workshop
www.phylcampbell.com

The Life of

a Boy with

Big Dreams

Willie Craddick Jr.

This book was written for teens everywhere. Life isn't all peaches and cream, but learn what you can and make your life a success.

The Life of a Boy with Big Dreams

Growing up over the years in my household was a rollercoaster.

My younger sister was dramatic and went overboard about everything. She was unmanageable. She managed to get her way about everything. My mother and sister act just alike. My mother used to use my younger sister's age for an excuse to all her wrongdoings because she was younger than the rest of us.

It was hard being the only boy in a family full of women. Every time we got in an argument, they would always try to team up on me and try to take me down. I did not have a voice for a while because I tried to keep the confusion down. When I got a little bit older, I started standing up for myself.

I held things in for a long time. But finally, I got tired of pushing things under the rug and I spoke my mind on anything I disliked. This helped me deal with things but really didn't help my situation.

Things started getting worse when I turned twelve. I used to argue with my mother and sister non-stop. Whenever I argued with either of my sisters, my mother always took their side. Over time I got tired of going through the same situations with them. I got tired of living with them. I used to be so angry and tired. There were times I did not want to come home from school because I knew what was waiting for me when I got home: the arguments and fighting. Things never got better: they only got worse and worse for me.

Most days of the week I did not speak to anyone at home. That became a problem, because my mother got upset when I did not want to talk to her or either one of my sisters. I just wanted to keep my distance from them, though, because once you already do not like a person, everything they do makes you furious.

The last day of seventh grade was a terrible day for me. When the school day was over, I got on the bus and rode home. Once I reached my destination, I got off the bus and walked up the steep hill to my house. I came right in the house and went upstairs to my room. After a few minutes of being home, I was sitting on my bed in my room, and I heard very loud music from outside. My bed was next to the window, so I looked through the blinds. My mother driving up the hill in her car with the very loud music coming from her speakers. I could hear the rocks crack under the tires as she blasted up the steep hill.

I felt butterflies inside of me and I knew that day was not going to go great. My mother got out of the car, slammed the door, and opened the door to the house. I didn't expect her to be home, so I sat on my bed and waited.

"Junior, come on," she said in a tired and frustrated voice. She slammed the front door the same way she slammed the car door, and went back to the car.

Were we supposed to be going somewhere? Had she told me? I didn't remember. She normally would not come home after work to get me.

I came down the stairs, being careful to shut off all the lights as I went, grabbed my key, locked the front door, and got in the car.

She started yelling as usual. She asked why it took me so long to get in the car.

I said, "It was only two or three minutes 'cause I had to cut all the lights off so your bill would not run up."

She said "SO! You do not pay it, so it should not matter!"

I said, "You always complaining about the bill being high, so I wanted to make sure everything was turned off so it would not be high!"

And on and on we fought. Nothing I did was right by her.

We left to get my baby sister. When we arrived at her elementary school, she ran out the door. She was asking for chips and a juice as she jumped in the car. My mother went to a local store that was close to where she was going. It was in a not-so-good neighborhood. People called it "The Block" and you could smell the scent of drugs and all the smoke from people smoking.

As we were sitting in the car, my mother got out to get the chips and juice. People were walking by the car. My baby sister was yelling out the window at them.

These people had guns and were selling drugs -- anything could've happened while we were in that car. I told her to stop yelling at those people because they could do anything to us while our mom was in the store.

But my baby sister got upset with me and she hit me. I hit her back. I told her not to hit anyone intentionally and unless she expected to get hit back.

She hit me again.

So I hit her again.

Then she saw our mom coming out of the store and started crying dramatically.

With the window down, Mom heard my sister crying out loud. As she got in the car she started yelling at me. "What's wrong with my baby? What happened?"

I tried to tell her what happened, but when my sister said I hit her, all hell broke loose.

My mom tried to hit me – for hitting my sister -- without knowing the whole story. I told her there was a reason why I hit her. I told her she hit me first. She told me she didn't really care.

I deflated like a balloon. Someone let all the air out of me. It was the last day of school and the start of summer vacation, and all I could think about was that it was three months of being with my mother and my sister and losing every single fight every single time.

And I was trying. Trying to turn out the lights and help with the bills. Trying to keep my little sister safe from thugs. And my mom acted like she didn't care about any of that. She acted like she didn't care about me. Wasn't I her kid, too?

Did I look so much like my dad and did she hate my dad so much that she hated me, too? And every time we fought, I just wanted her to say, "I love you, I still care about you, I'm sorry you're having a rough time, I'm sorry growing up is hard." I wanted her to tell me I was worth something. I wanted her to yell at my little sister ONCE.

My mother was assuming the wrong thing about my sister and me because of our seven-year age difference. She thought I should let my younger sister get away with things because she is the baby of the family.

However, if my baby sister didn't learn at home, I knew she was going to be in all kinds of trouble in life. She had to learn that there are consequences to her actions.

We were riding back home, going down this bumpy road. I was mad. Sweat was running off my face because it was so hot. I was looking out the window with a big frown. I was very angry with my mother.

The whole way home, she was yelling at me. "Do not ever put your hands on her ever again!" she screamed at me over and over. She was going on bad about the situation.

I felt like we could never get home fast enough. I had a feeling that something was going to go down, but I did not know what it was. When we reached home I ran up to my room and slammed the door.

She came running upstairs to my room and I heard her clearly come to my bedroom and start to yell. I was so angry I yelled back through the door. But I didn't open it. Then after all the yelling we did, she was like, "I should whoop you, but I'm not because my boyfriend is about to come over."

I wasn't crazy about the idea of my mom having a boyfriend, but just then, I kind of felt relieved. I was so over arguing with her.

Five minutes later, Mom's boyfriend pulled up the driveway, parked, got out the car, and came into our house. They started talking and they went in my mom's room and they started arguing. About what -- I'm not sure.

And I'm not sure where he was when later that night my mom was like, "Y'all come on. I'm going to buy y'all some chicken."

Me and my younger sister did not mind because we were really hungry. We got in the car. I didn't stop to turn out the lights this time. I didn't even bother putting on my shoes. We were just going for a short drive in the car -- what did I need shoes for?

My sister and I got in the car and Mom started driving. She told me to look up the number for the chicken place. I didn't want her to be mad at me, and I was really hungry, so I did what she told me to do.

As she was driving, I was looking up the number and she kept hitting the curb. My sister and I realized that something was wrong with her. After the fifth or sixth time she hit the curb, I told her, "Let's go home before we wreck."

Loudly she said, "NO!"

I shouted back, "You're intoxicated! You do not need to be driving, because that's how people get killed."

I could tell she was upset with me, but I kept on. I said, "If we die, it's going to be your fault."

She said "Just look up the number and call them so I can order."

Maybe she wasn't as intoxicated as I thought. Maybe she was mad, too. And maybe she was hungry and once we had food, it would all be better. I started to call them.

She said, "Give me the phone."

I did.

She asked the employee if she could get ninety wings.

I said, "WHAT?! Mother, it's only the four of us. What do we need all that food for?"

The man on the phone said they could do ninety wings, but it would be over a hundred dollars.

I said, "No!"

But Mother said, "I can get that."

I said, "No -- because you already have to pay a lot of bills tomorrow."

We got stopped at a red light. She told me that she was tired of me trying to be her dad and telling her what she should and shouldn't do. And she told me she was tired of my attitude. Then we started arguing and she hit me multiple times in my arm and told me to get out her car.

I was very angry and upset, but I got out of the car and started walking with my bare feet. I ended up at a hotel. I went to sit down and I called my dad. I was upset and crying.

When my father finally answered the phone. I told him what happened and he was furious. He came and got me from the hotel, then we went to the police station and we talked to the officers and I had told them what happened.

The officers asked if I talked with my mother and I told them no. It had been a whole hour and she had not called me. The last time I talked to her was when she told me to get out of her car.

She finally called me while my father and I were talking to the officers. She was yelling and cursing me out. The officers heard everything. One of the officers took the phone from me and asked her what happened. She kept changing up the story and telling lies the whole time. After that, he told her he would come meet her when she was sober and in her right mind. I ended up moving in with my dad that night.

Mom did my older sister the same way a few years before, and that sister moved out and went to live with my grandma, so I was not surprised. I moved in with my father and things were great for a while. All I could say then was God is Good.

That night, I learned to never trust anybody, because anybody can turn on you at any point of your life -- even your parents. Moving in with my dad was great for the first few months of me living there. It was summertime and things were fun and seemed normal. We went fun places. We did things fathers and sons are supposed to do. We were spending quality time with each other. Things seemed to be going great.

But that didn't last long, and by the time school started again, my father was leaving the house on school nights and not coming back the whole night. Then he started dealing with different females and doing for them and not me. He would go on lots of trips with his girlfriends that did not include me. I understood that he wanted to spend quality time with his girlfriend, but he left me sitting at home by myself all weekend, every weekend. When he went out to eat during the weekdays with her, I was not included then, either.

One situation that really got to me was a week before a movie premiere, I asked my father if we could go that next weekend. he said we could. I was so excited.

I was thinking we were about to go see the movie and I was excited about it and then he comes in my room the day before and was like, "Oh. Change of plans. My girlfriend called and asked could we go out to eat and I told her yes."

I was like, "How you going to make plans with her when we supposed to be going to the movies?"

He said, "Yeah, I know, but we can always go another time."

I said, "There will be no other time because I won't be asking again."

And I meant it.

So a few months later, there was this basketball game my father had tickets to. He was supposed to go with his girlfriend but she told him she wanted to spend time with her family.

So he asked me would I go.

I said, "Yes."

Then, the day before we would have gone, I told him I wasn't going because I was going over my grandmother's house. He got upset, but I didn't care about his feelings. For a minute, he could feel how I felt when he was supposed to take me to the movies. And he was supposed to be the grown up. So I basically stood him up the same way he stood me up.

The first Christmas staying with my dad was the worst Christmas for me ever, because we did not do anything as father and son like we did over the summer. It was always him being over at a female's house and me being stuck at home alone. I seriously thought Christmas would be different.

I stayed over at my grandmother's house and I didn't receive any gift or even a call from my father. My grandmother was the only person who bought me a present. She tried her best to make my day and make up for my parents. But I was so angry because I had two parents that worked and made a good living but they were so caught up in love that they could not think about their child.

My grandmothers on both sides of my family were my go-to people, they comforted me and showed me the way to stay strong. Many parents do not understand that there is more to raising a child than providing for them. Yes -- that's the main thing when having a child is providing -- but you also have to have that physical, emotional, and mental attachment with your child. If you do not, your child can be missing that one piece that can destroy them inside and causes them to be depressed. There are families in the world that I envy because their bond with their children is the bond I wish I had with my parents.

One situation that occurred changed everything. My dad came in my room and he could hardly breathe. He said, "Junior, I think I'm dying."

I just burst out crying because I didn't want to lose my father. I was crying for a good minute then I told him to go sit down and that I would called the ambulance and they came and took him to the hospital. We got there and the doctor said that he would be okay, he just had a lot of fluid in his lungs.

His girlfriend came. She was a very nice, educated, and respectful person. She was very good to me. She brought me food and she made sure I was good. She was a great mother and woman. She stood by my father's side through the whole process of him being in the hospital.

But the day before the last day in the hospital with my father, they got into a huge argument. My father's girlfriend was very upset and she took me to get some food so I could have something to eat that wasn't from the hospital cafeteria. I asked her was she okay and she said yes but I knew she really wasn't.

Finally, she told me what happened and I told her everything would be okay -- that I knew how my father was. I told her she should do what was best for her because she did not deserve to be hurt because she was a great person.

She and my father used to break up and get back together. My father had a lot of infidelity issues. She told me that my dad's infidelity took a toll on her and she knew he was still in his same ways of doing what he wanted to do.

I told her I wasn't surprised because he did my mother the same way. We talked for a while and I told her how great I thought she was. She took me back to the hospital, told me thank you for everything, and left.

The next day we left the hospital and she took us home. At home, I got out of her car and went into the house. She and my dad were still sitting in the car, talking, and I guess she told him what I said. He came in the house angry and started yelling at me. Me and my father were arguing for a while.

I did not care what he thought because he was in the wrong and he knew he was. He'd got a good woman right there that came to his rescue when he needed something and he still treated her like nothing.

I never could understand my father. I watched him and knew I could not be like that. I watched him and knew that I was a person who stood up for what's right. I'm not the type of person that will excuse bad behavior from someone just because we are blood. I knew if he was doing wrong I had to call him out on it. I don't care if he was my family or parent or anybody.

My father didn't like that about me, he always thought I should stand behind him no matter what he did. This woman had a son my age and she took me in and treated me like hers. She deserved the best -- not the worst.

It wasn't like I hated my dad. I didn't. It was just that you have to do right by people. A few months after my dad and his girlfriend broke up, he went and got back with the women he first cheated on my mother with. There were a lot of women that my father went through, but it was this particular woman that he always managed to go back to. The first time they were together, he cheated on her and they broke up. The other times I'm not sure what happened because I was not around them then -- I was staying with my mother. They got back together after a few months of me staying with my dad.

Me, my dad, and she went out to eat and she was like, "Is you dad still a cheater?".

I burst out laughing. "How you not gonna expect him to cheat with you," I asked, "when he cheated on someone just to be with you?!"

She was way older than I was, but I had more common sense then she did. She kept seeing my father. And he went back to leaving me home alone. He would go out to eat with her a few times a week every week and I was not included. They would go on all these trips and I wasn't included.

I understood that my dad wanted to have alone time with his partner sometimes. That didn't bother me. But he still should have remembered that he had a child and she should have respected that as well.

I was left out all the time. Every holiday, I had to go over someone's house or stay home. I never spent any holidays with my father. When my father was dating all these females back to back, there was never any time for me. After a while, I came to my senses that my father did not care about the way I felt because he was always too worried about a female.

The weekends staying at the house alone while my dad was out having fun were not much fun for me. Thanksgiving and Christmas, staying at home while he was with her family, didn't even feel like they were holidays. I used the time alone to think a lot. I had a lot of things running through my mind.

For example, I used to think that he only kept me at his house so he would not have to pay child support.

Things just go really worse with my dad towards the second year mark of my staying with him. I started getting close with my mother again. I had forgiven her because I had a dream that something happened to her and I wouldn't be able to bear the pain. So I forgave her; I was always a momma's boy.

The second Thanksgiving of me staying at my dad's house -- that's when I started getting closer with my mom. I spent Thanksgiving with her. My father hated that me and my mother were getting back close; he was scared that I was gone move back with her and he would have to pay child support again.

The weekends my father did not want to spend with me, I was over my mother's house and that was basically every weekend, because my father was always doing his own thing. Then the weekends my dad did not have anywhere to go because his girlfriend would be out of town, he would try to do something with me. But he only wanted me when I was the last person on his list.

I used to tell him "No," that I was not going with him and that he could spend the weekends alone like I had to. I went over my mother's house and it felt like home over there again.

So first Mom. Then Dad. Sometimes my grandmas. And a lot of time alone. A rollercoaster. And not a fun one. I was angry and I was depressed and I was lonely.

With all I was going through, all I could think about was finding my talent so I could pursue it and be successful. I think about my future day and night.

I discovered that I wanted to be an actor on television. I always wanted to be on tv. I love watching different tv series and I always wanted to be on the big screen.

But also? I always loved fashion, so I wanted to start a clothing line. And I did. I started my own brand and created a clothing line.

I want to be a Hollywood star AND a business owner. I've had people – even family -- laugh at me and tell me I would not make it, but I'm very determined to prove them wrong.

Make sure you always have plans for your future and do not ever let someone tell you that you can't do something. People tell you that you can't do something because they did not succeed in what they wanted to do. Use their criticism as motivation -- that's what I do.

Before you know it, we will all be adults and then come the bills and doing more things adults do. Always follow your dreams and make sure you work hard. Once you're focused and determined, you will succeed at any goal you set out to achieve in life. Once I put my mind to a goal, I succeed at it because I've worked hard for it. Following your dreams is not easy.

For example: I wanted to start a clothing line and I thought it would be easy but it was it actually harder than I thought. It was very expensive, so I had spent each check I got from my job to by a little bit of stuff at a time. I had to pay someone to make my logo and I had to pay different companies to make my shirts. I was in for a wake-up call that was terrible, but worth it. I did not have money to hang out with friends, because I invested in my future. But I know it will all pay off. For this clothing line, I was broke for months and I had to work long hard hours each day just so I could finally launch it. It was worth the wait and hard work.

It is great to have my future planned out and be working for some of those goals I want in life. It's great because it has me motivated and I won't be wasting time doing crazy things I do not need to be doing. It's nice finally working on my dreams instead of dreaming about them.

Do not let your dreams slip between your fingers. It's not going to be easy achieving them. You have to put in some work to get the results you want. Life is short so do what is your passion. Acting and fashion are my passions. I just really want to brand myself and be a star. I know it won't be easy but it's gonna be worth the blood, sweat, and tears.

Teen Tips Part 1

I know we may go through things in life and you wonder how you are going to get through them or are you even going to make it. If you have faith you are going to get through the problems you go through and everything should fall in place. Life is not easy -- I've experienced some hardships but I've gotten through them. I try to always stay prayed up.

One thing I always did was my work and I always made good grades because I'm very motivated to be successful in life. My life has not been all peaches and cream -- I've hit rock bottom before. Here's more I've got to tell you about my life and what I learned from all of it. Maybe it will help you.

Anger

At school and outside of school, I see a lot of angry teens that are mad at the world because of what they have been through. I've been through a lot of stuff and I'm still trying to get through some things. The people I thought loved me the most hurt me the most. Made me question everything about them. There has been some family and friends that have caused me pain.

All this built-up anger started when I was ten. My parents divorced, my dad moved out, and me and my sisters were left with Mom. My older sister moved out when she was sixteen. My younger sister thought she could do anything and not get in trouble. I always got in trouble. Me and my mother did not talk for days and sometimes weeks. When we did talk it was mostly arguing because she used to be angry all the time for no reason. We were always at each other's throats. I didn't know what happened to my old mother, but I wanted her back. I hated the new person she had become.

My seventh grade year was one of the most terrible years of my life.

After my mom and dad divorced, my mother began to be more angry than usual. Every time she looked at me, it was like she was looking at my dad. Me and my mother did not get along for nothing -- we were always into it about something. Over some time, I became angry. I went to school angry. Every day I took my anger out on my teachers and students at my school. I used to talk the teacher and students any kind of way, and I used to treat them badly.

I've gone to school and put my hands on people when I was angry. I've cursed people out for the smallest things. One thing I had to learn was to take situations that I have been through and learn from them so I would not have to go through them again. I started to reform my life and I stopped letting people get to me. My anger issue used to be real bad growing up. I had to let go and let God. Being upset every day of the week for week and months is not a good feeling. I used to not want to wake up in the morning, but my anger issue taught me so much.

I was always the type of person to hide my feelings and let things build up inside of me until I exploded. Then I found a way to release that anger -- by writing and talking to God about it. It helped me a lot. I still have a lot of pain and anger in me, but I'm working on it.

Things are changing in my life from how they used to be because I started to let go. Anger will control you if you let it and it will cause you do to things that are not like you. You have to make sure you find ways to release anger in positive ways and not the wrong ways. I used to fight people to let my anger out when I was younger, but getting kicked out of school was not an option for me, so I had to grow up and find better ways to deal with my anger. Whatever you are angry about, face it and find ways to release it before you regret doing something bad.

Bullying

There was this one kid at my school that go bullied for not having name brands and a lot of materialistic stuff. The boy who bullied him was one of my close friends -- until I found out he was bullying this boy. Every day in class my old close friend used to bully him but I was not near them. I used to sit across the room from them and I was so focused on my school work that I did not pay attention to what other kids did in class.

The bullied boy came and told me about the bullying one day in the hallway. He said that my close friend was bullying him every day, calling him names because of his clothes and stuff. I was shocked, because I do not surround myself with that type of people. So I confronted my old friend and I was like "why are you bullying this boy?"

He said, "'cuz he not nobody. Look at him."

For a minute I just stood there, looking at this guy that I used to be close with. Was this what he really was? It took everything in me not to beat the crap out of him right then. Still, we got into it at school -- we shouted at each other -- because I do not stand for people getting bullied -- especially not by my friends. I can't stand people who make somebody feel like less of a person because of what they do not have.

This situation had me so livid that I was about to actually fight him, but I was learning to control my anger, and knew fighting him wouldn't help.

My old friend went around school saying he was going to beat me up and saying little stuff to get under my skin and make me mad. I didn't care what he said about me. But It was the fact that this boy who was bullied came to me for help -- plus he was going through stuff at home, too.

My friend had gone against everything I stood for. I had been so focused on school and grades that the bullied kid had to come tell me himself. But once he did, I wanted him to know he was taken care of. I wanted to send a message to all bullies that I didn't stand for that. Even if you had been my friend. Because my friends wouldn't do that.

Every day I used to wait for him to come to class so I could beat the crap out of him, but he would avoid coming to class because he knew I was waiting for him. I knew I needed to let that go and move on. And I really tried. But he was really getting under my skin and really making me mad. And he didn't stop bullying the other kid.

I talked to the boy who was getting bullied and I told him to stay strong and not to let words hurt him because someone was always going to have their something to say. I told him there's always light at the end of the tunnel and that he just had to get through the hard things first.

But even though I was trying to help this bullied boy and ignore the bad behavior of my old friend the bully, the bully wouldn't leave the other kid alone and because I wasn't fighting him, he started giving me the business, too. I could avoid a lot of nonsense by being on my side of the classroom, but now that I was paying attention, I saw the bullying get worse and worse. The teacher didn't do anything – even though there was no way she didn't see anything. And it just made me so mad. It was so unfair.

I watched the kid who was being bullied and I talked to him often. He told me things got so bad he was considering suicide. And still nothing was happening and no one was doing anything to help this kid. And every time I tried to check the bully, I got in trouble.

This went on for a few months. I would try to let things go and just talk to the kid. The bully would target both of us -- but mostly the kid -- and mostly while I watched. I would get fed up and check him. I would get sent to the principal's office. Or the principal would call me down. Just me -- never the other kid. It was like there was something going on, but I never figured out what it was.

I sat down with the principal of my school and he told me not to fight him and to let it go and I told him I did. The principal said if I fought him I would get suspended for ten days.

I knew I could not afford to get suspended because in high school if miss one day of class you can leave that class with a 91 but when you came back from missing a day of school you could be at a 75 quick. I had a 3.8 GPA. My grades are very important to me.

The next day, I walked past the bully in gym. When I got far away from him he said some slick*[1]. So I went to the gym locker room

---

[1] Some slick -- something said under the breath or out of earshot to cause suspicion, confusion, hurt feelings, or anger.

and got his stuff and dumped everything out of his book bag, including his phone. The phone was already cracked, but I made it useless.

I know that you should never put your hand on someone's belongings but I felt like I owed it to the boy who got bullied by him. I wanted that boy to feel the same pain he was making the boy he bullied feel. I was wrong for touching his things, I made a mistake and I own that. I should have just beat the crap outta him off school property and not during school hours.

But I feel like if you are a bully you need to be beaten up because bullying is never okay. I knew my hitting and fighting was usually caused by being messed up inside -- like the way I was angry all the time when my parents were splitting. But I didn't think about what caused his. Only that he was tripping because he had stuff the other boy didn't -- like that phone. Before I broke it.

But after I broke his phone, we had a meeting with all of our parents for mediation. There were witnesses to my breaking the phone, and I had been warned not to fight the boy. So of course there were going to be consequences. I didn't fight him, but school didn't care for the way I did instead.

However, the school counselor wanted us to squash things. They knew I was mad that teachers and a lot of people knew what was going on and they didn't do anything to stop him from bullying. They knew I didn't just break the phone because of what he said to me.

The meeting went left very quick – which I didn't expect but I probably should have -- when my parents started arguing, not with the bully's parents, but with each other, in the middle of the meeting with the mediator.

My father was taking the bully's side before he even heard the full story. My mother had my back the whole time -- even though she was not happy I broke the boy's phone. I knew I was wrong for breaking the boy's phone and I owned that. But my mother could see why I did it and she supported me.

When the bully's mother told my mother that her son was better than me, I burst out laughing. I told my counselor to pull our grades up. When she pulled up both of our grades, I said, "if your son is so much better than me, then why is he failing all his classes and I got a 3.8 GPA?"

She could not say anything for a bit.

Finally, she said, "I should press charges, but I'm not because you are a child."

But I think she really knew what her son was all about. If she pressed charges against me for the phone, the bullied boy's parents might have pressed charges against her boy for the bullying. I may have been wrong, but at least I had a good reason. He didn't have anything like that, but was just being mean.

When we left the mediator, I really saw who was there for me and it was my mother. She called me out when I was wrong and that is what I respect. Still, she had my back the whole time.

From this situation I learned that you are responsible for every action you make and it's never okay to destroy someone else's merchandise. I was wrong in every aspect of that situation and I took full responsibility. I just wanted the bully to feel the same pain he was causing the boy I was protecting. If the principal did not warn me about the ten days of suspension I probably would've beaten the crap out of the bully -- but I'm glad he warned me because if he hadn't, I would have lost everything. I also know that physical altercation is never okay and there are different ways to solve a problem like this. But at that moment in time, I did not care because I hate bullying with a passion. In school I was never really bullied because people knew I did not play those types of games, but I know for sure they said stuff behind my back. They just knew they better not come to my face with it.

I'm a wiser person now. I told the person that I was trying to protect that -- in life -- people are going to say what they want. You choose how you take what they say. You have to stay strong and do not let people treat you any kind of way. But don't go too far the other way -- don't be the bully -- either.

You can choose to use their words as motivation or you can believe them and look stupid. You always have to stand up for yourself in life and stay true to yourself.

Drugs

Drugs are a problem that people focus on at school. All I hear about drugs from classmates at my high school who used them is that they are life and people should try them. I don't agree.

You have to think wisely before you use drugs. I know many kids I grew up with that changed because they started using drugs once we started high school. They started doing drugs because their friends did them. I have had friends do drugs and ask me to do drugs and I tell them NO! because I do not put nothing in my body I know that could harm me. People let their friends persuade them into doing drugs, but nobody can persuade me to do something I do not want to do.

I know people at my school that started doing drugs and they changed for the worse. Their outer appearance changed and they just changed as a whole.

There was this one boy I knew who tried drugs for the first time and he went crazy.

People do not realize that people who sell you drugs can put something in your drugs without you knowing that can harm you worse than the actual drug would. Everybody's bodies react differently to drugs. Your friend might can smoke, but if you try to smoke you could die because your body type is different. So you have to be very careful about what you put into your body.

In the process of doing drugs, you hurt loved ones and you harm yourself. You can kill your organs slowly or quickly -- depending on how much you consume of one drug and how your body reacts to it.

I hear people say you're going to die anyways, and I say I'm not trying to die anytime soon. When I die, I do not want to die from something stupid like drugs. Some teens at my school drink and drive and don't realize that if they hit a person on the road and kill them they are throwing their whole lives away, too. I try to tell people not to drink and drive, but they do not listen. Once they hurt or kill someone they gone be in jail and they gone wish they would have listened. You should never try drugs.

Forgiveness

Forgiving people is not my thing. I hold grudges towards people because I want them to feel the same pain they put me through. If you've hurt me I won't talk to you for year or for the rest of my lifetime.

For some reason I did not believe in forgiving a person. If they crossed me once, there will not be a second chance for them to make me look stupid.

My mother does not care for her side of the family. When she was growing up, she went through a lot of horrible situations. She grew up in a dysfunctional home -- the worst, according to her. So my mother does not communicate with her side of the family.

Her mother was doing a lot of outside things and she was not there for my mother. Her father was not there, either. She did not find out who her real daddy was until she was five. Then, he wanted to be there, but could not because of some situations.

My mother went through a lot of personal abuse and physical abuse. My mother did not have a father figure so she went looking for it in the world. Then she met my father and her world changed. In my father, my mother found everything she needed -- she thought. She looked up to him and I think she thought he was always going to be around. When he wasn't, it was like she stopped trusting anybody for a while.

My father grew up basically fatherless -- his father was there every now and then, but not like a father is supposed to be as a father. As a result, his mother raised her four children alone. She went through a lot of physical abuse, but she is standing strong as a great woman. She gives me a lot of support and encouragement.

When I was going through terrible times -- with my mother first and then my father -- my grandmothers were there for me. I struggled with forgiveness and if it was not for my grandmother on my mom's side, I would have never forgiven my mother. I did not speak to my mother for two years because I wanted her to hurt. However, I forgave my mother because I had a dream that something had happened to her and I could not bear the pain if something did happen to her. I would regret it. Now, I try to convince my mom to forgive her mother.

Me and my father have not talked for a year and I do not plan on speaking to him ever again. I know I need to start forgiving people because it will help me release anger and stop letting them have power over me. I just do not believe if someone hurts you, they deserve your forgiveness. You don't have to forgive anyone for anything. If someone you really loved and trusted hurt you, you don't have to put yourself in that situation. They should have known better than to put you through that.

On the other hand, I have to remind myself that forgiving people is not for them -- it is for you. Forgiving a person is not an easy task but it can and has been done before. I know you might have been through a lot of stuff but you have to forgive for your own sake. That doesn't mean things between you are perfect. That doesn't mean forgetting and being stupid around them. But that means not letting anger at them consume you anymore.

People have done me wrong in many ways and I'm still working on forgiving them. You can forgive a person but you do not have to forget. It can be your friend, your mother or your dad, or any of your family members. Do not let them feel like they have power over you, do not let them think they won just because you will talk to them. Forgive and let God deal with them. People are going to hurt you. It is a part of the learning experience with life, but everything will be okay and everything will work out in your favor.

Friends

Almost everyone has friends (unless they don't want them). But there are all types of friends you should know about.

You have the loyal friend that cares about your success. Then you have the friend that envies you and wishes for your downfall – sometimes that you are blindsided by that one. That one isn't really your friend, but sometimes you can't tell until your heart is broken and your trust is gone.

Friends come and go out of your life, but the people that are supposed to be there will stay through the good and bad times. Now those are friends.

Some people only talk to you only if it is beneficial for them. These people are funny to me, because they seem like they care about you but then they are also somewhere doing evil things behind your back -- just wanting to see you fall.

Then you have the fake friends that seems to like you. You think y'all are cool but then they talk about you behind your back. I've had many friends that turned their back on me or they changed for the worse and we grew apart. I came to high school with a lot of friends, but now I only have about four people that I can really call a friend. Not all your friendships are going to last forever and that is because you have to worry about you and how you are going to make it and survive. Very few friends are going to pay your bills and make sure you are good when you need them. You see who your real friends are once you hit rock bottom. You will see who is there for you when you have nothing. People will go and come all throughout your life. You have to choose people who you think will be loyal and have your back.

I tell myself all the time I do not need friends to be successful because after high school everyone is going to go their separate ways and they are going to do their own things. That's why I tell people to focus on themselves and their success, because if they do not, nobody else will do it for them.

Making Decisions

Decision making is a major problem among teens -- even myself. We tend to not make the best decisions. When I'm very angry, sometimes I do not think clearly and I make the decision that I think that is best in the heat of the moment. But it's difficult to make the best decisions when filled with anger. When I'm not angry and I'm thinking, I make the best decisions. But I still need some work.

Basically, teens like me -- we sometimes make decisions based on how we feel or based on what our peers do. If some teen friend drinks beer, many others would make a decision to do the same. There are, however, some teens that have their own mind and do not let people influence them. That's me.

I'm my own person and I would not choose to drink because that is not me and I was not raised to think drinking was OK. You always have to make the decision that is best because if you do not you can suffer consequences. You might lose privileges, your grades could suffer, making it harder for you to go to college, you can be sent to jail, or even worse.

People at my high school make poor decisions like skipping class and cursing out teachers. I make the decision to go to class and do my work because I care about my future. There are sometimes I want to check a few people -- but I do not because I know it would not end well. When I'm angry, I do not think. But I try not to not put myself in situations where I repeat mistakes, so I try to avoid the things that make me angry -- like when people talk bad about me.

I know people who are so used to making bad decision it's become a habit for them. Do not make bad decisions a habit because if you do you would end up in a place you do not want to be in.

There are all types of decisions: decisions about life, decisions about relationships, decisions about choices at school, college, all kinds of things. Any time you're put in a position to choose a decision, pick the one that is best for you -- because only you know what is best for you. If you make a mistake, that's okay. Just make sure you learn from the mistake and do not make the same mistake twice. If you make the same mistake twice or three times, then that's a problem you need to fix.

I used to always look up to my older sister. Whatever my older sister did, I wanted to do it too. When she used to fight I wanted to fight, when she used to talk back to my mother I did to. She was bad in school, so I was bad in school too -- until I started seeing the consequences for all the things I was doing. I was getting in school suspension like every other day.

I used to have to go talk to counselors. They used to tell me all the time, "Willie, you have great grades. We are trying to figure out why you do the stuff you do." I was trying to fit in. I was trying to fit in with bullies who didn't get checked and teachers who acted like they didn't care.

When I was younger, and angry all the time, I used to do bad things just to impress my friends. I thought making them laugh might make me feel better. I used to get kicked out of class. At the time, I thought it was cool.

I came to my senses and realized doing wrong things was only going to lead me to one place or the other -- and those places were jail or dead in a grave. Acting bad was not going to pay my bills in the future. Impressing my friends was not going to help me in my future, either. I had the learn the hard way.

I used to have an uneducated way of thinking when I was younger. Now I spend my time talking to people that I see going down the wrong path. I tell them the same thing I needed to learn. I try to get them to see if they do not change now it might be too late later on in life. You can always change but all the opportunities you threw away may not come back to you. People do not understand after high school life gets so real out here in the world. I'm in high school, but I see the effect life has on people after high school.

Every choice you make will be your responsibility. No one will be held accountable for your actions but you. Life is nothing to play with -- especially after high school.

However, sometimes fitting in is a good thing. Most places, you have to work as a team to get the job done. Being a team player is very important. At the same time, you should always be comfortable being yourself. If you aren't, why not?

The best way of knowing if you are fitting into the crowd in a good way or a bad way is to know what you want in life. Make a list of your goals and dreams. Then think about a hard question someone has asked you. If the person wants you to do something that doesn't go along with your goals, get outta there! A lot of people want your time and attention for them. Be your own BAE.

Mentors and More Education

Sometimes in life there are not many people that will show you the way of life. There are only a few people that showed me the way; many people wished for my downfall instead. Even the people that was supposed to love me the most – some of them prayed for my downfall. I had to learned that not everyone wants you to succeed in life.

If you have a mentor, make sure they are someone who is trying to succeed in life and guiding you the right way. Do not let someone mentor you that is not living the right way themselves. If you try to let someone mentor you who is going down the wrong path, nine times out of ten, they are going to lead you right with them.

A few mentors I had in my life were my eighth grade math teacher, my grandmothers, my mother, and God. My eighth grade math teacher taught me that not every situation needs a reaction. My grandmothers taught me to always pray, and put everything I was going through in God's hands, and everything would get better. My mother taught me the importance of school and being successful. She is one of the reason why I'm so motivated to be successful. There were times I had to mentor myself, and many would say that is impossible but it is actually every time I got off track I had to remind myself why it is important to stay on track and succeed.

Learning can take you a long way. The more you know, the further ahead you will be in life and the more money you will make. I'm not just talking about education, I am talking about life skills, too. Make sure you take advantage of every opportunity that comes your way, because you never know who you could meet, you never know where each opportunity will take you. I have taken many opportunities in many fields that I really do not want to pursue in the future -- but I took them because I never know what could happen.

During those different experiences, I have met many people that want to be in the same field as me in the future, and I have learned so much from them.

If you want to be successful, you have to network. That means meeting many people and finding out about them. Maybe they can't help you, but if they can't, they probably know someone who can. I found out that people get ahead because they know people more than they know stuff, so you should meet as many people as you can, and give them respect. Because you never know what could happen.

But if you don't treat other people with respect, they won't help you and you won't be able to learn anything. You might stay exactly where you are while everyone else moves past you to a better life.

Learn as much as you can about your field or anything that has to do with life because the more you know the better off you are. I used to try to figure things out on my own for a long time, but when I started asking questions, things became much easier for me.

Always fill your brain with as much knowledge as possible. I figured if I learned what I needed to learn know when I start getting deeper into my career I would be fine because of all the knowledge I learned. But the more people I meet, the more I know school education is not nearly enough. Reach out to people, and ask questions. Ask as many questions as you need to so that you understand whatever it is they were put in your path to teach you.

Even if you think there is no way someone could help you, ask anyway. Maybe your janitor went to school with the person you want to work for. Maybe your teacher's kid plays soccer with someone you'd want to shadow for career day. Don't be afraid to talk about your dreams and ask for help making them into goals and into reality.

There is nothing wrong with learning and doing your research. You have to do that. You have to find out all the information you can from books and the internet and school. But the internet can only give you a list of places and what people said about them in reviews and stuff. The internet can't tell you if the reviewer is a good person or if they have the same opinions as you or what situation is best for you. But people who get to know you can tell you places to go and places to avoid. And because you learn about them, respect their opinion, and trust them, you can save time not going down wrong paths because they can tell you the right ones and help you get there.

Money

As a teen money becomes a huge aspect for you, because the thing you would like to do revolves around money. Money gets you where you need to go, and want to go. I love hanging out with friends, we would go to restaurants, shopping, and places where they had fun roller coasters. All that cost money. My parents stop giving me money, and I got tired of asking them, so I got a job.

There is nothing like having your own money that you have worked for. When I started my own clothing line, I took all my checks for three months straight and invested in my clothing line. It was not easy, because there were things I wanted to do on top of that, but I could not do them, because I used the money for my clothing line.

Starting a business costs money, the amount depends on what you're starting. Once you have an Idea write out a business plan, and follow it so you know our going in the right direction with your business. Check off each goal you have to accomplish. Money was one of my major problems when pursuing my business; I was tight on money for a while.

I had to work long hard hours outside in a farm for hours just so I could get money. Working on the farm was my job for two years. I needed to save up $600 dollars so I could get everything I needed for my clothing line.

When I was in the process of starting my business, I didn't have time to hang out with friends, My life was always work and school.

The days I was off work, I slept in, and did lots of research. I could not balance hanging with friends, going to work, and school. It was just too much and I could not risk losing money hanging with friends.

Do not get me wrong -- all my friends are important to me -- but sometimes you have to handle business. I'm getting older, not younger, so I needed to start making some moves so I could have a platform.

Make sure you always research everything that has to do with your business, go out and ask questions ask people who have the same business you -- or something similar -- to give you tips. Ask lots of questions so you know what you're getting into.

Parents

As teenagers, some of tend to not listen to what our parents have to tell us. I have been that person where I did not listen to my mother or father, and when they tried to tell me something, I did not listen, so I had to learn the hard way. I'm lucky the situations I had to learn from were not too harsh. I learned my lessons quick.

Sometimes parents are wrong, and they do not like to admit they are wrong. Just deal with them not owning up sometimes. There were times my parents did some crazy things and when I called them out on it, they would deny doing them and they would be shocked at the same time. I had to learn that your parents want tell you nothing wrong, but if you just listen, you'll be surprised on what they know. I was raised differently from many other kids who shared my surroundings. The way I was raised formed me into the person I am today. My life could've been worse. It could have been worse because of the times I didn't listen and it could have been worse because my parents didn't always understand the whole situation.

It's hard to know when to listen and when not to if you're in the heat of the moment. But if you can step back a beat, often the thing you should listen to seems like common sense. Things like not fighting at school, not breaking someone else's things, not doing drugs, not giving in to any bad kind of peer pressure. But you also gotta know when you just can't bow down to somebody. You gotta know when enough is enough and you gotta be ready to take action when you have reached your limit. I've needed to learn better ways to do this.

But some parents just do not care about you finding your limits or figuring out how to be an adult who can take care of yourself.

In those situations, all they care about are themselves. Some kids feel lost in the dark or -- in a word -- lonely. If their parents only care for themselves, who is going to take care of the kid who's all alone?

I thought having a child would be the best blessing in the world.

I guess not for some parents. I used to feel unwanted and I definitely did not have a bond with my parents -- me and my mother had a tight bond before the divorce and now we are tight again, but there was a time when we couldn't even look at each other without getting into it. When I moved in with my father, the bond was strong until he started meeting all these different women. Then he had no time for me -- he was always out with them on dates and dinners and whatever else more they did when he was away. I used to just come home every day from school and just go straight to my room. I did my homework, showered, brushed my teeth, and went to bed. My dad didn't even check on me. My dad used to come home, take a shower, and leave for the whole night during the weekdays. On the weekend, he used to leave Friday and come back Sunday, leaving me by myself. The bond we had went away, over time but quick.

If you are a parent, or thinking about being a parent and turning the tables, I learned that you should always spend quality time with your children. It's more to having a child then feeding them and clothing them. You have to have a bond with your child.

I'm not going to follow anybody who doesn't care about me and my big dreams and my goals. And I'm not going to let anybody trample someone else, either, because that is not what we are put on this earth for.

Peer Pressure

Peer pressure is a major topic that should always be discussed. Peer pressure is when you are pressured by someone to do something you're not sure about or something you do not want to do. In high school there is a lot of peer pressure that goes on. I mostly see seniors pressuring young freshmen to do something they do not want to do or are not ready to do. I hear about many boys pressuring young girls to try sexual things they do not want to do. The boys convince them that it is okay and the girls fall in their trap. Peer pressure is never okay!

Be on the lookout for pressuring situations. Sometimes you may not even notice it. I had some friends that are girls and they used to tell me they used to do things for their boyfriends just to keep them. They did things they were not comfortable with. They did these things because they loved their boyfriends.

I used to tell them no matter what type of situation it is, you should never let someone convince you to do something you do not want to do. I used to also say if your partner loved you enough they would not make you do something you're not ready to do. They should understand if you are not ready.

I would never make a female that I care about and that I'm in a relationship with do something she is not okay with doing. DO NOT let someone take advantage of you in any way, because if you let them, they would do it over and over. Many people are victims to peer pressure each year. Just make sure you are not in the same situation and make sure every choice you make is because you wanted to and not no one else.

You are your own person. Remember that.

Relationships

I'm in high school and relationships are a major topic because it is that time where everybody wants to be with someone and not alone. There are two types of relationships: healthy relationships and unhealthy relationships.

In high school, I see both types of relationships. The relationships I hate seeing are the unhealthy relationships. Innocent females fall in love with these older boys and they take advantage of them. There was this one relationship where this boy was doing what he wanted to, and he had a great girlfriend. He used to hit her and tell her if she ever left that he would commit suicide -- so that's why she stayed in the relationship with him.

One day in school he hit her and a lot of boys beat the crap out of him. He deserved it. (I did not witness the fight personally, but later someone showed me they recorded it and I watched that.) If I was there, I would have beat the crap out of him, too, because you're never supposed to put your hands on a woman. Not ever. That is just out of line.

That is why I try to tell females do not rush into a relationship! Just because your friends are in one does not mean you have to be in one. Someone will eventually gravitate towards you -- do not go out looking for something because you will end up looking in all the wrong places.

The best people in my life were my grandmas. My dad was not the best role model I could have. I want to be everything I felt he wasn't. I don't have to wait until I have my own wife and kids to know how to respect people in a relationship. You don't, either.

You should always treat a woman with all the respect you can give a person. You are supposed to treat her like a queen, not use and abuse her heart and emotions. Women are God's greatest creations. My father does not see that -- I do not know why -- because he played more females then I can count on my fingers. Playing with a female's heart is the worst thing you could ever do. I know that because I've seen the pain my mother went through over and over. That pain damaged her forever and it changed her forever. That type of pain plays with a woman's self-confidence and self-esteem. It has a woman thinking she is not good enough or her looks are not up to par. Once you are dishonest to a woman, that changes her whole outlook on men. Once a woman has been cheated on or abused in a relationship, she is going to believe every man is going to be the same.

My mom and dad had problems that got worse each and every day that had a mental toll on my life. They fought physically and verbally and it had gotten terrible.

They fought every day because my father cheated on my mother many times. My dad cheated over and over and my mother took him back every time because she believed he would change. He said he would, but he never managed to. I used to always think "why would my mom be so deceived to even believe him after the first time he cheated?" I used to tell her not to take him back. But she did anyways.

She told me, "Junior when you are in love with someone, you become blindsided because of the love you have for them."

I used to say, "Mom, when I get a girlfriend I won't be blindsided as you."

But I was wrong. I experienced what she was going through when I was in the seventh grade and I had gotten my first real girlfriend. We were together for nine months. Then I found out she had cheated on me. I was very devastated. I cried and cried for several weeks. And for several weeks I said to myself, "How could she do this? Where did I go wrong?"

Then I did the same thing my mother did. I took her back, over and over, thinking she would change.

But she never did.

I was so blindsided by the love I had for her. Over some time, I got over her, but she taught me a life lesson: to never give second chances when a person cheats on you.

When they say "I'm sorry," they knew them cheating would hurt you, but they still did it anyways knowing it would hurt you. That lets you know where you stand, because if they loved you enough, they would never do anything that will hurt you.

I do not believe in taking a cheater back anymore; once a cheater always a cheater. Your partner knows what they are doing when they are cheating on you and they aren't worried about how you would feel if they did the cheating.

I know I'm young and it's a part of the life experience, but being cheated on is the worst life experience you could go through in my opinion.

Like, how could a person you love so dearly treat you like that? I guess some people do not have the same heart as others. I would not dare cheat on a female that I'm in love with. That is just crazy and stupid. I could not put another woman through the same pain my mother went through. She raised me and my sisters to be faithful and loving.

What I tell myself and males like me is to focus on your education and do the right thing. Everything else will fall in place. If you go out looking for something, then that is where you mess up. Then you wonder why things are not going the way they are supposed to.

Your success is something you should always focus on first. Get your main priorities in line. That's going to take you where you need to be in life. Then everything you want (besides your success, which you will have) will fall in place as you achieve your goals. You do not need a partner to survive. So worry about the important qualities of your life and you should be good. You have a whole lifetime to think about a relationship.

Respect

Respect is something a lot of us teens need to read up on. You have to respect people to get far in life. If you're not respectful you want get a job and you won't get far in life – that's something I learned quick.

When I was in elementary and middle school I did not listen to no one and I was very disrespectful, but that all changed once I got to high school because I knew in a couple years I was going to be an adult and I could not let my attitude hold me back from my full potential in becoming successful. I had to change quick.

Once I changed, I saw things start to fall back in place for me. People wanted to help me achieve my goals and life became better. When you show people respect that make them want to help and support you, but when you disrespect a person that make them not want to be around you and not help you. There are kids at my school that curse teachers out and disrespect them and they wonder why their grades are not where they need to be to pass.

When a teacher disrespects me now, I try my best not to disrespect them. But if they do it continuously, that's when I have a problem with them. I start not liking them and when I lose all respect for a person, it gets bad for them. I do not care who you are -- if you respect me I will respect you. I'm not a disrespectful person anymore -- but I can be. I try to be nice and respect all people but some people take my kindness for my weakness. Most kids at my school they disrespect a teacher just to be the class clown and make everybody laugh them are the types of people that are not wise because a teacher has more power than we think they have. You should always respect people in your life if you want to be blessed with all the things you want in life. Being successful is all about who you know in the business.

Respect Yourself

Self-respect is major, because you always have to respect yourself. Do not abuse yourself, because that only brings you down as a person. If you do not respect yourself no one else will, because people would be like "well they do not respect themselves so I will not respect them." Do not let people disrespect you either, because if you let them get away with it they will do it continuously. Do not let what people say about you get to you. Let people talk. I know many teens that I go to school with have a self-image problem --including me. Many of my fellow classmates talk about their weight and other parts of their body. They say how they want things to be different like their weight, if you want to lose weight you have to be dedicated to losing weight it is not an easy task. However, do not change the way you look because someone else does not like it. People always are going to criticize everything a person does, so do what you want to do. Do not do things you are not comfortable with. Stop trying to impress others. Always do what is best for you and not others because if you don't, no one else will.

School

Teens, stay in school, education is the best thing they have offered us.

I know kids that I attend school with that take education for granted. They skip class and do not turn in assignments and do whatever besides doing the right thing. Most kids that I know that skip class are in these gangs and walk around school trying to be a thug and think it's cool. They smoke and do drugs on school campus. Most of the kids that are in gangs that I know and see? They just be following the crowd trying to act tough because they see their peers doing it. Some people do not have a mind of their own. They do it just to be like everybody else.

I never understood why some people would want to be like someone else with no future. Or in jail.

I had to learn that I was blessed with a mind. One thing I always did was my work. I have a 3.8 GPA and I'm looking at college. I always made good grades because I'm very motivated to be successful in life.

When it is time for the upper class to graduate from high school some of them do not make it to graduation. The graduation rate today is above eighty percent. Our school graduation rates have risen over the course of the last five years, when we were below seventy percent[2]. The kids who do not graduate are too busy running the streets and not going to class.

---

[2] Clarke County School District. (n.d.). Retrieved August 14, 2016, from http://www.clarke.k12.ga.us/news.cfm?story=698

They start crying in May when they realize they won't be getting a diploma. And I laugh because they was not crying when they was skipping class; they was not worried about graduating when they was not turning in work.

They skipped their classes every day and they failed their grades. They just lost so much self-respect trying to be like someone else. Some of the people I know even dropped out of school just to run the streets like their friends.

Those teenagers do not understand that the decisions you make in high school will determine your future. If you mess up, you could change your whole life forever. That is why you have to be real careful about what you do, then ten to fifteen down the road you going to wish you never made that decision to skip class, you going to wish you never made the decision to try to be someone else. School is important because you have to graduate to get a great job to make a great living.

I know a lot of grown-ups that wish they had taken their education more seriously. They found out it is hard living paycheck to paycheck. They can't pay the bills they have, much less save and build a foundation that will protect them. If you lose your job, but have a foundation, you still have money to pay your bills until you find another job. But if you don't build that foundation, and don't have a high school diploma, it is real hard. Your diploma and your foundation is basically a backup plan so you can survive and not have any worries. You cannot be a child forever so that why it is smart to start planning your future and achieving some of your short term goals.

You have to focus on your life and not someone else's, because there is going to come a time when you have to take care of yourself and your own household. When that day comes, fitting in will not get you where you need to be in life.

Self-Control

Self-control is very important for many reason. If you do not have self-control you can be locked up or something even worse, and you could lose everything you have worked for because of some simple situation that you let get out of control.

Self-control is when you have control of yourself in difficult situations. For example: if you are arguing with someone, make sure you do not take it as far as physically attacking them, because arguments that turn into fist fights usually do not end up well. However, if you keep your composure, then you have self-control.

I had to learn the hard way that people aren't always going to agree with what you have to say. While you should always respect their right to have an opinion (just like they should respect yours), just walk away if you know the situation won't turn out well. Having self-control can save you from a lot of problems. You have to think before you act. I used to act, then think, and that's where I used to mess up, because once you choose to take actions into your own hands there is no coming back.

The second semester of seventh grade, I had a lot of anger in me. Growing up in a divided household was draining and it just made things worse for me mentally. Because of my anger, I became a big bully. There was this one time that semester that people had been telling me that this boy was calling me names.

I was young and not using my head, so I went up to the boy and started beating him up. I did not fight him because he was talking about me, because I know people are going to talk about you until the day you die. I fought him because I had so much build-up of anger from home and I thought fighting him would release some of it. But it just made things worse for me.

Consequences may vary. It depends on what you did when you reacted. If you put your hands on someone first, then you have messed up, because physical aggression can come with a lot of charges and consequences. I was punished with three days of suspension. I had to get zeros for classwork and it really hurt my grades. After that, I knew nobody else was worth getting in trouble over. I knew I had to change myself. So I did.

Violence is never the answer to any situation. There are times when I really want to strangle a person, but I have to think and ask myself: "Is it worth losing everything I have worked for? Over something so stupid?"

And I try to let it go and walk away.

Self-Reliance

I learned that you should always have your own and not ask nobody for nothing. I've always been a hardworking person but from the ages of one to thirteen, I could not work because I was too young.

Until I was a teenager, my father used to give me money with no problem. My mother did, too. When my parents were together, before all the fighting that led to their divorce, they made sure they took care of me.

When I needed money for trips they always made sure I had enough money and I was taken care of. I went on all the school trips -- all my parents asked of me was to keep As and Bs, which I did. I never made a grade below a B because I worked hard in school. School always meant a lot to me -- my mother made sure of that.

My mother made sure everyone in our household made good grades and was doing the right thing in school. If we did not make good grades all the materialistic stuff we liked was taken away.

But when my parents divorced and I was a teenager, I would ask one parent for something and sometimes they would say yes, but then not have the money. And sometimes they would say no, to ask the other parent. And I hated going back and forth and not having what I needed. I hated having to ask.

I had this competition to go to in Macon it was called the Agriscience Fair. I had to create a project and present it in front of judges. I went and competed. I needed $150 to go. My father was supposed to give me $150 to go, because he said he was going to give me the money. A week before I left for the trip my father came in my room and was like I'm only giving you $50 and I'm like "what?"

He waited until the last minute to tell me that. So I called my mom and asked her if she could give me $100 and she said yeah -- remind you I was still staying with my father during this time. She said she would give me the money and she did. A day before the I was about to leave for Macon, I asked my father for the $50 he had agreed to give me and he said he was not giving it to me and to ask my mother for the rest. I'm like, "are you serious?" She gave me the rest with no problem. My father was shocked, because he thought she wouldn't be able to afford to give me the rest.

I went and I won first place and that was my second time winning so I went to the national level once again in Kentucky. I competed in my eighth grade year for the first time and we competed at the end of the year at state level, and I went to Kentucky in my ninth grade year in October for national level. I competed again at the end of my ninth grade year at state level, and I went to Kentucky in October of my tenth grade year for national level.

After winning I was happy and proud. My mother believed in me. I came back home to my dad's house. I did not tell him about me winning. I just set my award on the table to let him know I still did it – and I did it without him.

Christmas came around again, I thought me and my dad was going to spend Christmas together. Well, I thought wrong because he chose to be with his girlfriend and before he left he came in my room and was like, "you better find somewhere to go because I'm going out."

I was not surprised, but Christmas is a holiday that you are supposed to spend with family. Every holiday was the same thing living with my dad. We never did anything together after that first summer. On Christmas of that year, I tried calling my mom, but she was out of town already. She had asked me the week before if I wanted to come with her, but I said "no" because I thought my dad would change for once and spend some time with me on Christmas. I was wrong once again. It's not fun when you are never thought about.

When I used to go over my mother's house she would tell me to just pray for better days. When I used to stay with my mother, when we got into it, I used to yell that I wanted to stay with my dad, but I learned the hard way that he was not better.

During the end of my freshman year, things were ending with me and my father, too. When I got home one afternoon, I went straight to my room. My father came in there and was like, "since you feel like your mother is right, from now own you tell her to get your haircuts and buy your clothes and feed you."

I did not entertain what he was saying because I was tired of arguing with him. I'm thinking in my head, *what's the sense of me staying with you if you are not going to do your job as a father?*

A week later he came back in my room and was like, "You're moving back in with your mother this summer."

I said that was fine with me.

He had been telling me weeks before that we were moving in with his girlfriend. Both of us.

He asked me what I thought and the first thing that came to my mind was NO. How was I going to sleep in the house of the woman he cheated on my mother with? Second? If she gets mad or yells, if she gets into a heated argument and she throws both of us out on the street and we have nowhere to go – then what?

Gladly I did not have to worry about that anymore, because when I moved in with my mother for the summer things changed. On the last day of school of my ninth grade year of high school, I packed my things and went over my mother's house. Back at my mother's house things went well. My birthday came and father came. He brought me some money, but the only reason he did was because he was feeling guilty. He knew he had been treating me wrong. I took the money and I played like I forgave him. But then he never heard from me again.

No one's not going to treat me any kind of way and then expect me to have a bond with them. He called me a week after my birthday cursing me out and calling me names because I did not call or text him. His birthday came and Father's Day came and I did not call or text him, because he spent two years treating me like I was not his son.

To this day he wished he never counted me out. He calls my mother every day asking how I'm doing and asking how I'm doing in school. When he was angry and cursing me out, he said he would not call or anything because he did not care. I still don't know if he has changed or if he just doesn't want to be left out.

My grandmother called me and told me that everything would be alright and God would take care of everything. I told her I was not shocked he brought me something for my birthday. But I just wanted him to remember what he did and all those times he went out with some female and left me alone.

Me and my grandmother had gotten close while I was staying with my mother. She did not call my father for his birthday or Father's Day either, so he came to her house and even to her job where he followed her around and cursed her out. And I watched him and I wondered, how could he curse at the woman who gave birth to him and raised him?

She made sure he graduated high school and went to college, and everything, and that's how he treated her. Every time he did not have a place to go he came to her house. She fed him and made sure he was good. She did not ask him for any money.

He cursed at her because he was mad because she did not tell him "Happy Birthday" and "Happy Father's Day." He told my grandmother he did not know what was wrong with me and her and he said some very disrespectful things towards her. My grandmother was shocked -- like why would he even do this to her? -- but I knew this was coming.

Before my father came over, my grandmother had cooked dinner for me and my cousin. My auntie came over and she chatted with my grandmother and then she and my grandmother came into the living room and she asked me if I had talked to my father.

I told her, "NO."

Then she said, "Y'all need to stop it."

I told her, "I do not need to stop nothing" and I told her, "You need to be telling him he needs to stop it. I have not done nothing wrong."

Then she went on trying to give me a speech about my dad and how I needed to stop it.

I stopped her and told her to hold on, that she could not tell me what was going on, because she didn't know the whole situation. Only the people that stayed in the household know what was going on between me and my father. Then I told her that she only listened to what my father had to say. I asked her why she didn't realize he was a liar when he wanted to be.

She insisted that she believed what he said.

I told her, "This the same person that sits right here at grandmother's house with me and talks about you to my grandma your mother." I wanted her to see, even just once, that she was being played by him.

She wouldn't see it. She just kept insisting that "we stop it," meaning that I should apologize. It was like just because my father was the adult, I was wrong and he was right. But people that are right don't go around biting the hands that feed them and leaving the people they care about behind. People that are right don't choose dates over their kid. Not at Christmas or any other time.

I was so angry. I told her she knew my father was only nice to people he thought he could get on his side. That she knew he could play people and that he was playing her. I said, "but you taking up for him though."

She said "I know your dad talks about me."

She was going to say more, excuses and stuff, but I cut her off quick. I said "Well you cannot tell me nothing about nothing then."

She got mad and said, "I'm not about to argue with a child."

I said, "you're right, because you do not know what be going on and that is your best bet!"

I do not care much for my auntie anyway because she always got something to say. She called my grandmother and was yelling at her because she did not tell my father "Happy Birthday" and "Happy Father's Day." My grandmother told her she did not call because she did not feel like he had been a father after the way he treated me.

Then my auntie started yelling at my grandmother, and I lost all respect for her. When she needed money, she called my grandmother and my grandmother always came through for her. I could not believe that my grandmother had two kids that treated her so badly. At least she has two other kids that are perfectly nice with steady jobs and all that. So why are some people so messed up?

My grandmother did so much for me growing up. She always took us on adventures and different fun places growing up. She still takes us places. She did so much for us. There are grandmothers out there that do not even want to be bothered with their grandchildren. My grandmother is not like that and this how her kids treat her. My grandmother took us to different adventure parks and water parks -- basically anywhere we wanted to go for fun. She's such a great woman, and she does so much for the family but this is how she always got treated for years. She tries so hard to try to bring the family together and tries to make it work.

My grandmother believes there's a reason why they treat her the way do, I tell her all the time I told her there's no reason in the world they should treat you this way, you are their mother and you were the only one who raised them -- with no help. But my grandma insists she failed somehow when it came to my father and my auntie.

Family should not treat family like the way our family works. My father and auntie used to get on the phone for hours and they would talk bad about the whole family. I watched and listened to them, thinking that if you have someone in your family struggling, you should not make fun of them or talk about them behind their backs, you find ways to help them if you have the power to help. You do not watch them fall. Why sit on the phone and dog them out when you can just help them? If you have that power use it! That's the type of family I have. Most of them do not care about nobody but themselves.

As soon as I was old enough to get a job, I did that so I wouldn't have to ask my parents for money every time. It was hard, but it was worth it.

My teen tip to you is to make sure you always work and keep a job so you do not have to beg people for money. When you borrow money from people they always got a story to tell everyone they know.

Now that I have gotten older I tell myself if I do not have the money to get it on my own I won't be getting it until I have the money to buy it. Now that I'm old enough to work, I do not ask nobody for nothing.

Everything I have, I have purchased with money I earned -- clothes and shoes and more items I have. Having your own money that you worked for is the best feeling in the world. No strings attached to money you didn't borrow or take from someone else, even your parents. People throw up in your face what they did for you and I hate that. But now that I have my own income, I do not worry about that any more.

<u>Setting Goals</u>

Setting goals is very important. I try to set as many goals as I can to keep myself going so I won't be wasting time doing something not important. I'm a teenager and before I know it I'm going to be an adult and out on my own. That's why I started a clothing line -- so I could have a foundation.

When I leave to live on my own, I won't have to call home asking for money to eat while I'm in college. I'll be living on my own – not calling to get help with my bills. I worked and took my paychecks and invested in this clothing line because I love fashion. And I wanted to have my own brand. One of my long term goals was to work hard enough to make money for the clothing line and get everything started and I did.

If you want to be successful, you have to set short term goals to reach the long term goals. Many successful people started off small and they built their brands. You have to work hard for every goal you set out to accomplish. It is not always gonna be easy -- success takes hard work and dedication.

There are times when you want to give up, but just stay strong and have faith. That is what I do with every goal I set out to accomplish -- I accomplish it. I know a list of people that want their success handed to them -- and I laugh at them.

Some say it is easy to be successful, but they are in for a wake-up call. In the long run, they're gonna see what it really takes.

If you really want to be successful, you have to work hard and stay focused. Do not let people talk you out of your future. They are the people that, because they did not make it, they need to talk down about other people that they see the potential in making it. They are just miserable people that are mad. People still talk down on me when I tell them I want to be an actor – they say I can't do it and that I can't be successful. I'm going to prove them wrong. I'm going to prove them wrong like I've done before.

People said I couldn't be successful at a job. But I was. My first job was at this farm funded by the school district – the Young Urban Farmer Program. They taught us how to farm, how start a business, and how to profit from it.

We had to write a business plan and conduct a business. During the business classes, they had local business people come out and tell us about their experience -- how they started a business, how they kept it going.

They also taught us how to sell a product for a reasonable price and still make money, because you do not want your product to be so high where people won't buy it. When we worked on the farm some days, our managers taught us how to weed. The correct way for weeding is to pull all the roots out of the ground completely. If the weeds aren't pulled all the way out, they will come back faster.

We learned how to harvest different types of vegetables and different types of fruits. Most of the vegetables were easy to harvest, some were a little more difficult because you did not want to bruise them.

Every Saturday we sold the vegetables to the local community in a farmer's market. Other local people and their businesses come out and sold to the local community, too. The market had clothing, prepared food from different cultures, garden-fresh vegetables and fruits and more.

I sold natural tie-dye shirts. I would use fruits and vegetables to tie dye plain white shirts. I used blueberries, beets and spinach to make the different colors of dye. The shirts sold well; it was good income for me. Most Saturdays I sold out of t-shirts.

The Young Urban Farmer Program showed me a lot of important steps to life. However, program funding was cut from the school district, and the other students left. I stayed and kept selling – and selling out of -- my t-shirts every Saturday.

The funding cut took a toll on me because for a while the farmer's market was my only source of income and I didn't see being a farmer for my whole life but I wasn't sure I could do the business plan part of it yet. I had to put my clothing line on hold and get different jobs and keep making the tie dye shirts to have income to put to my clothing line. Tie dyed shirts were alright and sold well, but they were not what I wanted to represent my brand. I learned that it is always safe to have more than one source of income because you never know what could happen.

Stress

Stress is a common problem for most teens, including me. We stress so much over relationships and school and whatever else is going on and going wrong in our lives. Stress can to lead to high blood pressure and depression.

I'm always stressed and overthinking situations. I'm constantly overthinking my future and thinking -- what if I don't make it?

Then I'm always stressed about my past and what I went through and I constantly have flashbacks on the things I went through. I cannot get over them. I've been working on trying to get my head together because some days I wake up thinking about my past and then other days I'm stressed about my clothing line and getting everything together.

Sometimes stress is something you cannot control. You have to just have faith that everything will work out right. I thought that I would not get through this pain I went through. But I did. I came out strong. There were nights I cried and cried and could not sleep because I was stressed out and tried but I got through it.

I'm still in the process of getting over what I went through in the past, but it is going good. I'm not in the space I was a year ago. A year ago I was still going through a lot with my dad. And there still is a lot going on with that, but it's all good. I'm still learning the let go and let God.

Stress will eat you alive if you let it. Just believe everything will be okay and you will be fine. Just have faith. My grandmas reminded me that I had faith for years and they kept reminding me how it really works. Just pray about your problems and everything will work out for the better.

Life is going to throw you a lot of dodge balls. You just have to just make sure you're ready for anything life throws at you. Sometimes in life I would question God.

"Why I have to go through this?"

"I'm a good person and I do the right thing, but ...?"

and

"Why me?"

I learned that you never question God and his plans. There is always a reason for God's every move in your life. God would not put you through something he knows you would not be able to handle.

In some situations in my life, I see why God did what he did. It opened my eyes to a lot of things and it taught me so much. Some things I still wonder about, but it is a learning process. I will figure out someday when he is ready for me to figure out. Sometimes God puts some tests in your life to see if you learned from your past situations. There were some times I would make the same mistake over and over because I was not seeing the bigger picture he was showing me. I learned that if you are going through some things put it all in God's hands and he will take care of it.

I used to try to deal with my problems on my own but I learned real quick that it is okay to put everything in God's hands -- let God deal with people the way he wants to. I used to try to get revenge on all the people that hurt me in my life, but I learned to let God do his work and he would take care of everything. Situations that you go through can break you apart and just make you feel like giving up. I've been there. Because I've been there, I know there will be a time in my life that I will visit that state of mind again, but I just have to let go and let God.

I'm not perfect. I really have to work on myself and my anger. I know what I have to do and I'm still working on it. I only had a few friends I can talk to about situations that I went through and they understood me. I have had a few teachers that used to wonder why I acted the way I did, but once I told them my story they understood where I was coming from. Still, there were times when no one could understand me, and I had to find some common ground within myself. I would tell myself it is okay if no one understands me. The only people that would understand me would be me and God. You are going to go through situations in your life that you would have to go through on your own with no support system and no one to vent to. So you need to figure out how to be that person for yourself.

When I needed to vent, I used to just write things on paper. Sometimes I wrote some things I would like to say to get them off my chest. I just threw it away right after I finished writing. That was a system for me that helped me get through some situations. Like any solution it didn't always work, but I was surprised how often it did.

There many other ways you can reduce stress in your life, but I often chose writing because it was the best way for me. Then I thought I could help other people if I wrote a book. So I wrote them all down again.

Now that you have read my story, complete your own Teen Tips to help you through the ups and downs of life's roller coaster.

Teen Tips Part 2

In this section of the book, write your own thoughts about helping yourself be successful in life. Whether you create your own book someday, or whatever goal you aspire to, writing down your thoughts is one way to start you on the path to achieving your dreams.

There are some questions and lines to get you started, then there is blank space for thoughts, ideas, lists, sketches – whatever you feel like adding to the pages.

Anger

What things make you really angry? What can you do when you feel that way?

_____

_____

_____

_____

_____

Decisions

Have you ever been faced with a decision?

How did you decide what to do?

_____

_____

_____

_____

_____

Drugs

What would you do if close friend wants you to try some kind of drug?

_____

_____

_____

_____

_____

Fitting In

How can you stay real to yourself and your goals? What's going to be your biggest challenge

_____

_____

_____

_____

_____

Forgiving Others

Who do you need to forgive in life to be at peace with yourself? How can you make it happen?

_____

_____

_____

_____

_____

Friends

What qualities do you expect your friends to have?

_____

_____

_____

_____

_____

Mentors

Writing about and talking to people about my problems helped me act out less and do well in school. Who do you have that you can talk to about things you are going through? What kinds of things would you tell someone if they knew or cared enough about you to ask? Write some of them here. Nobody's going to judge you.

_____

_____

_____

_____

_____

Money

Where does the money you spend come from? How will you protect yourself if that source goes away?

_____

_____

_____

_____

_____

Parents

You can't choose your parents. But you need things from them. How can you work with them to get what you need?

_____

_____

_____

_____

_____

Peer Pressure

Sometimes you need to put a plan in writing so you know you have something you'll stick to if you're put in a tight situation by peer pressure. So do that now.

What is your plan if:

Your partner wants you to have sex?

_____

_____

_____

_____

_____

OR

You forgot to study the night before, and someone offers to give you the test answers for ten dollars?

_____

_____

_____

_____

_____

_____

OR

Your friend is making fun of someone's non-label clothes, and wants you in on the joke.

_____

_____

_____

_____

_____

OR

Everybody's going to the keg party Tuesday night, but you've got an algebra quiz second period Wednesday?

_____

_____

_____

_____

What are some other situations you might need a plan for?

_____

_____

_____

_____

_____

Relationships

What are you looking for in a relationship?

_____

_____

_____

_____

_____

Respect

Who is someone you respect? What qualities
do they have that you admire?

_____

_____

_____

_____

_____

School

What can you do to stay focused in school?

_____

_____

_____

_____

_____

Self-Control

When you do feel like you are out of control? If
you can't control the situation, what can you
control? How can you help yourself let go or
walk away?

_____

_____

_____

_____

_____

Setting Goals

What are your goals for life after high school? What can you do now to put those other goals within reach?

_____

_____

_____

_____

_____

Stress

What causes you stress?

_____

_____

_____

_____

_____

How can you cope with any of the stresses
you have?

_____

_____

_____

_____

_____

Suicide

Have you ever thought about killing yourself?
Who could you talk to if you needed someone
to listen and help you?

_____

_____

_____

_____

_____

You

What advice would you give another teen?

What's stopping you?

_____

_____

_____

_____

_____

About the Author

Sixteen-year-old Willie Craddick Jr. is proof that if you work hard, you can make your dreams come true. Willie wrote this book to inspire and encourage others to follow his example and work hard for their dreams and goals. In addition to writing this book, Willie created his own clothing line, shopbashed.com, maintained a GPA of 3.8, and worked two jobs. He was also a member of FFA. His FFA experience includes being a two time Agriscience Fair National Finalist.

He plans to go to college and major in business. Then, he plans to move forward to pursue a career in acting.

Visit his website shopbashed.com/williecraddickjr.

Follow Me

Twitter: @williecraddickj

Instagram:

@williecraddickjr

Facebook:

@williecraddickjr

Thank you for buying this book and helping support my dream.

Keep supporting me.

SHOP!

shopbashed.com

/williecraddickjr.

Made in the USA
Charleston, SC
29 September 2016